AMERICAN ROADS

Freya Manfred

AMERICAN ROADS

THE OVERLOOK PRESS / WOODSTOCK, NEW YORK

Acknowledgment is made to the following publications for poems or versions of poems which originally appeared in them. *Anima; The American Poetry Review; Beyond Baroque; Bloodroot; The Boston Phoenix; Carleton Miscellany; Earth Journal; Field; Great River Review; I Sing The Song Of Myself; An Anthology of Autobiographical Poems,* Ed. David Kherdian, Greenwillow Books/Wm. Morrow & Co.; *Hanging Loose; Modus Operandi; Momentum; Moons And Lion Tailes; New Letters; Out Of Sight; Poetry NOW; raccoon; Stinktree; The Spirit That Moves Us; Stone Country; Sunday Clothes; South Dakota Poetry Anthology,* Ed. Linda Hasselstrom, Lame Johnny Press; *Traveling America With Today's Poets,* Ed. David Kherdian, Macmillan & Co.; *Women's Poetry,* Anthology, Ed. Ellen Rosser.

The author wishes to thank Paul Foreman, Editor of Thorp Springs Press, who published some of these poems or versions of these poems in *Yellow Squash Woman,* 1976, softback. Thorp Springs Press, 3414 Robinson Avenue, Austin, Texas 78722.

The author also wishes to thank The MacDowell Colony, Peterborough, New Hampshire; and Yaddo, Saratoga Springs, New York, for residencies which made possible the writing of some poems in this book.

Published by The Overlook Press, Inc.,
Woodstock, New York, 1979
Copyright © 1979 by Freya Manfred

Library of Congress Cataloging in Publication Data

Manfred, Freya.
    American roads.

    I. Title.
PS3563.A468A8   811'.5'4   79-14972
ISBN 0-87951-100-1
ISBN 0-87951-103-6 (de luxe)

For Tom Pope

CONTENTS

I

SOARING FRIEND WHO DOESN'T EAT

I have a soaring friend who doesn't eat,
who's thread and bone.
An airborn kite,
she turns her taut face toward me
in high wind,
and nearly disappears.

She wisps home after a walk,
sharpened by wind,
for a cup of pale tea.
She will not eat ham,
turkey, a smelt, by god!
Won't open her mouth,
let white teeth
crush shrimp, lap sauce,
shine with the grease of fowl.
She finds sadness, sadness
in the wombs of grapes.

When she calls
I won't go out.
I'd rather dine alone
than watch her watch me eat.
I'm suspicious she hasn't
a potato to stand on.

Who sucked the marrow
from her long bones,
made her peck
high and low through wind?
Who fed her such
rare hatred
that she'll starve us both
rather than remember
how she grew?

STORY OF A FRIEND

You first meet
a friend
naked, in the woods.
She invites you to swim.
A submerged rock
cuts one of you,
so you build a fire
and staunch the blood with lily pads.

Later, in flannel pajamas, she talks.
You listen as if watching
a fire at hearth:
it's not what she says
you remember, but the heat,
the brilliance, the changes
measured
the full length of your body.

You tongue her words
like hot scotch
until fumes
surround your head.
She relates a dream you've known
backwards since age three.
Two can walk
in the wound this dream opens.

A shadow flickers
on the wall behind your friend,
as male as she is female.
Near your hearts
the veins curl
in identical patterns.

When you're sick
and you travel rigid, into space,
your friend hugs
what's left of you.
She cooks your broth and tea
until you're ready
to reacquaint
with earth's strangeness.

Your love is confirmed
when your friend returns from a trip
and bores you with dull details.
She mumbles answers
to your personal questions
and snores into her pillow.
She knows you'll ignore her answers,
and find them someday
in one of your own poems.

THE FRIEND WHO SHARES MY HEART

Wounds glow
beneath her bandages.
She can't hide
her journey into
the mouth of the forest.
I'm hot on the trail,
blood on my teeth.
She cheers the ritual.

We speak
in a hurricane's eye,
though objects smash on all sides.
We lean into each other,
hands forgotten around tea cups,
eyes linked
above the delicate whirr of blood
in our temples.

Though we seldom meet,
the time between
is a corridor
leading into our lush dream houses.
We gather
all that should have been
mothered in us,
and give it suck.

She grows
until she gets her first teeth,
and bites her way out.
She doesn't forget
the part I played
in her creation,
her foundling mother's
cries.

IN SEASON

Nothing left
to October
but pick apples,
count the last Cosmos.*
I tighten my belt
over a flat belly.
Dry leaves
tick
tock
the bottom of my boots.
A dark animal
        I don't recognize
travels over the hills,
breaking its way west.

Winter.
Outside, the bones
of a long blue rattlesnake
flail the window.
My friend
tucks an afghan
around me.
She nods over the teapot,
robin warm-breasted.
Fat turkey crackles
in the oven.
        We discuss
the dreams of dogs,
how air bubbles keep, in ice.
Red blood rises
in my womb.

*Plant cultivated for its showy flowers.

In spring
I float off
sipping Bock Beer.
Ravenous, unpredictable,
I travel two states in one afternoon
to locate a pileated woodpecker.
I return to perch
on my friend's balcony.
Her hair flies wildly
around her skull.
Silent, I brood
over sap, blood,
in the dark
turning to bone.

Summer.
I ignore my friend at parties.
We pass each other
on green lawns,
and pass again.
Cheeks girded with
watermelon beards
we bite
into rubies.
       At midnight
leaves on the lake bottom
turn over and over.
I seize her in my arms.
She looks into my eyes.
My blood
turns to milk.

THE WHALE

When the young whale leaves her mother
and dives into one whorl of the sea,
blood retreats from her tail
toward head and heart. Her skin
thickens, white with diatoms, scarred
with rings where lampreys' mouths
            have sucked.
Darkness electrifies the water on all sides,
silent and black as newly-drawn blood.
        She is startled
by an unfamiliar knock from someplace near:
it is her heart
trying to get close to her,
tolling in circles through slow flesh.
                    . . .

The wrinkled brows of other whales
remind her of the folded face of earth underwater.
They are so large and sensitive, a light touch
sends a quiver along their whole length;
        so faithful
that she may play in their shadows for years,
at home with her labyrinthic body and heart,
        springing, like a redwood tree,
from the roots up.
                    . . .

She sifts plankton and krill
from a million drifting sparks,
devouring in reverie, a carnal meditation,
as if suspended in her own saliva.
   She follows the edge
of an offshore island down. Blue fish
ride each other like dragonflies. Red fish
puff in and out, like lungs just ripped from a body.
The island is attached to the ocean floor
by a thin tendon of basalt.
The earth's plates shift, the floor creaks.
   A moon-sized land mass
   splits open its rust-colored womb,
   rises beneath her
   like the top of a giant's skull.
                    . . .

There are fewer whales every day.
Some, wild in the ringing emptiness,
run aground in Florida with a sick pup,
refusing to leave until it dies, too late
to swim themselves free. Cold wind
drones on the domes of their heads.
Like hills which have slid from their height,
they shudder, crack, and dry,
crushed by their own weight.

                    . . .

The whale gives birth in warm water,
where the thick folds of the calf's brain
grow tolerant and flower.
The whale floats as the calf sucks,
        muttering to herself,
adding to the epic
which will not end at her death:
chording into the blue ear of the sea
phrases intimate and familiar,
which re-echo, years later,
in the songs of other whales.
                . . .

The whale misses the long naps of land creatures,
who rise from the ebb of dreams
where they fell asleep, astride an oak.
        The whale wakes deeper than where she fell asleep,
and doesn't sleep alone, or for long.
        Soon there's no difference
between sleeping and waking,
as if a certain beloved dream had entered
        everyday life,
each day arriving unmapped and unplanned,
part of her dream's choice in choosing her.
        The whale's underwater sleep
is like clouds when the earth inhales them,
turning to rain just before dawn,
whetting the heart for a journey.

THE JOGGER

On the beach a girl
is giving birth to a whale.
The whale is three-quarters out, nose first,
slick as rain on a black rock.
The girl's eyes are round holes, like those
cut into shale by sharp white shells.
Face down, she stares into the rooms
between sand grains.

An older woman jogs down the beach,
muscles knotted, elbows high.
She stops and soothes the girl's tight neck
with the pads of her thumbs.
The hairs on the girl's neck
rise in terror: the jogger's
mouth is a whale mother's maw;
the jogger breathes like a whale mother blowing.
The laboring girl retches,
as if the jogger were a soup made of spines.

The jogger trots down the beach.
When she is as slender as a tooth
in the mouth of the bay,
the girl heaves the whale's tail
out, at last.

As the newborn tunnels
into one whorl of the sea,
the emptiness under the lips
of the new mother's womb
is leviathan,
black as the Pacific trench
when underwater eyes do not shine,
    deep as someone calling her voice
    back into her throat
    from across a continent.

GOLETA BEACH

On a rocky point two miles from town
an empty wheelchair faces the Pacific.
In front of the chair, hand prints and two knee furrows
mark the sand for fifteen feet,
erase at the water line.
A small brown terrier
curls on the wheelchair,
chin on paws, ears tipped toward the sea.
    Water green over water grey,
    white slash of spray over black rock,
    kelp snakes winding, hiss.

Waves break on triangles of rock a mile out.
    Below,
the man from the wheelchair swims
into a coral bed the color of frozen blood.
Strong shoulders pulling,
legs trailing loose as sea worms,
he bubbles, somersaults,
sense of balance a whorl.

The terrier on the wheelchair
turns three times and drops to wait.
How long will his master hold his breath?

The master,
soft white legs rippling back
like the feathers of an angel,
arches underwater:
one last flight
through his blue heaven blue:
dives, loops,
the dark water
molds his legs into a merman's tail.
    Water green over water grey.
    White slash of spray over black rock.
    Kelp snakes winding.

WOMAN AT SEVEN CORNERS, MINNEAPOLIS, MINNESOTA

The green lamp post on the corner
is ridged and scratched. It stares at gloom
with four, spare, gold eyes.
She strokes the post. Her lips move.
She peers up, frazzle-white hair falling from a bun.
She wears black shoes like boats,
one extra-thick sole for her short leg.
Spittle on her lips, flying spittle in the air,
she exhausts herself informing this post:
She visited the freshman dormitory
at the University, with a present.
Her boy found her waiting downstairs,
puffing, sweat above her lip.
She pressed stale brownies in a sweater box
against his oak-hard stomach.
Her boy frowned, "Oh Grandma."
Rattled, she remembers winter.
She ran out of sugar,
the cat's eyes clouded, the phone never rang,
trucks roared past all night.
She offers to treat her boy
to fresh strawberry pie, fifty cents a piece,
but where is he going, in his springy tennis shoes?

NIGHT NOISES AT THE COUNTRY ASYLUM

I

Jane Hall
sweet sixteen
terrorized by her father,
who is an insect shaped like a rocket,
meets me in Ward Nine.
She grips my left arm,
cries long tears like threads
when she reads my poem about women.
        "Your words understand me."
She wants to write words
but her handwriting is too large for paper.

She tries the white walls:
        "Son of Something
        Son of Touch
        and Kiss of Moon
        is all we Have,"
        says Jane Hall, already playing the piano.

Her hair smells
like the yellow snakes
pushed out of a pimple.
But her breath is peppermint;
her fingernails clean
and cut.

Jane sails to psychotic prairies
where one lone loon pipes up,
"ha ha ha ha ha"
on one lone lake,
laughs over a shoulder
"ha ha ha ha ha"
at the furiously paddling boatman
who can't locate
the loon's new hiding place.

Jane hears night noises all day.

II

What do night noises know, Jane?

What stories will they tell
about things
painted with the blood
of sacred animals,
things unlawful,
razor crazy,
sad?

"An ear
inside an egg
inside a blood vessel—
a small body
on nightwatch
inside me—
listens.

Drunk, near Mexico,
I can't remember his face.
Ashamed he could be anyone.
Afraid he could be someone.
Locked in an Iron Egg
in the Hospital of Ovens,
I hear one of my selves
sucked out of me
by fire.

Nurse Superior
waits near the latch,
growing claws and teeth.
Doctor Number One unzips
to exhibit
his miniature American flag."

III

I drive away from Jane
with my car window open.

Mingle-mangle night noises
come from piles of dead ears.

None of the night noises
recognize each other.

Each blares
one contrary note
into the dark country garden.

Buried trumpets
blast
inside flower buds.

Clenched wiresprings
explode
inside bloodcells.

Flowers of blood
seep through the blackness.

MARGARET'S MOTHER

Margaret bows over the bed
of her 75 year old mother
in the Old Folks Home:

"I'm here, my angel."

"Oh my sweet girl. Oh my sweet girl."

> I take the hand
> of Margaret's blind mother,
> pull her arm from under the covers.
> It unfolds
> like the wing of a chicken,
> springs back into fetal position
> when I let go.

> I might lift her into my arms
> any minute,
> hold her between my breasts
> like a dangling, long-legged frog.
> I might surround her dry bones
> with my juices,
> push my fleshy hills
> against her body flats.

For lunch Margaret's mother refuses
chewed hamburger, mashed potato,
faded asparagus
and milk.
She eats
chocolate pie with whipped cream.
She flaps her mouth
when Margaret promises to find
bourbon and water,
smiles
when the bourbon hits her throat.

Margaret's mother
is handsome:
bones jutting beyond flesh.
Her thin legs are raised.
I cannot imagine her shrunken womb
giving birth to Margaret.
The objects in the room
have been dying since August
when Margaret's mother last touched them.

An old man with no-teeth
sits on a couch by the door
tilted at a 45 degree angle,
exactly as the nurse left him
when she went to answer the telephone.
He can't pull himself up to 90 degrees,
or drop into a horizontal position.

    I don't mind sitting with Margaret's mother.
    Dying looks possible.
    Letting spider webs dry, and blow free.

    Margaret says
    she can smell death in the room like acid.
    I cannot detect it.
    This is not my mother.

UNIDENTIFIED FLYING OBJECT

I managed to get it to approach
    last night,
because I forced it into shape.

It shuddered into view,
naturally tall,
sculptural,
silver-grey tidbits
    strung along a glowing spine.

Prodding,
    I found crushed umbrellas,
    highway rest stops,
    sleepy lagoons with walls of vines,
    and nests made of car hoods lined with bear fur.
My death, made of shelters.

    Hands came flippering:
    yellow callused, powerful as monkey wrenches;
    freckled and sun dry, old sandpaper.
    My friends' hands,

    in a language I recognized,
    pried at the bone twists
    of the giant sculpture
    until it fell apart.

    I felt the wellrush of blood from a cut;
    I heard the song of bone as it dries;
    I smelled the breath the dirt breathes out
    when you crumble it in one hand.

    My throat made the sound of an oarlock.

    We all kissed. We all kissed.

WOMAN OF THE WARS

A ship sights a broad-shouldered thing
swimming alone in Antarctic water.
Men prepare for battle as reports come in:

She wears an egg-shaped helmet.
All the moles on her body are painted gold
and have small flags stuck in them,
flags of Greece, of Spain, of Russia.
Birds of transparent turquoise
flicker in her eyes,
make flights to her brain
carrying silver arrows in their beaks.
The knife charm on her bronze necklace
points toward her throat
where juice flows steady from a red slit,
streams to her breast tips,
freezes into bloodstone.

When they come near, her mouth spreads,
and they hear a sound.
The earth's door in space is opening.

SHE-THING

She sees things:
    his thigh, the aspen grove,
    the quiver of water
    in wind.
She sees things
that move behind other things:
    his words,
    the quiver of shadow
    in skull.

    Will these
    make up her left side,
    fill her heart with blood?

Her left side is the name she gives
to the woman
who has been walking earth
    thirty years,
threshing pale wheat
    with long arms,
noting the things she's seen,
feeding them into
    her footsteps down the road,
noting at times
the hitch of a missed beat.

    She worries
    where the things she can't watch anymore
    will go
    and what will happen to the woman
    the things watching her see,
    and what will happen to the man
    she sometimes seems to be.

She wonders
can she grow back
into the smooth rock her stomach was:
    back
    before she had to sing
    about things
she was no longer one with.

MY LEFT HAND

My left hand is not helpful like my right hand.
It does not assist much with eating, working, self-caressing.
My left hand writhes and undulates in moonlight.
It loves the pale juice of white flowers that melt at sunrise.

My left hand is my secret.
Sometimes it doesn't show up in photographs.
If I exposed it, someone could shoot it.
It could be sucked into the mouth of a boa constrictor.
My right hand would fight back and spit.
I often cover my left hand with my right for this reason.

My left wrist itches when I am near a man I despise
who excites my body. Only laughter dispels the itch.
I laugh because my right hand tickles me like a fierce broom
and my left hand tickles me like a deep-tonguing eel.

My right hand could talk politics, eat hot dogs, and climb
the Empire State Building.
When I dream about my left hand, it is a dolphin.
It glides under water, chanting songs to children while they sleep.

I will be an old woman in a red cotton dress riding a bicycle.
Behind me I will tie two wicker baskets filled with tulips,
ducks and quick dogs, a small garden quacking and panting
behind me.

I will wear rouge made of cherries on my cheeks and a yellow
sunflower on a garter snake chain around my neck.

I will eat seeds and peach pits and celery hearts and drink
elderberry wine in stables full of straw and cobwebs.

I will scratch the cow's back and the horse's ear and sing
off-key to them, "Bringing in the Sheaves," and "Mint Julep."

I will carry a pearl-handled revolver in my cardigan sweater
pocket, loaded with sunflower seeds.

I will tell more huge purple lies than thin white truths, so
people who have small eyes will open them wider.

I will campaign for the man who has the darkest and softest
beard for president, or else I will marry him.

I will grow as many wrinkles on my body as I possibly can,
and I will throw my two floppy wrinkled breasts over one
shoulder when I play basketball.

I will live in a house made of stained-glass church windows.

I will put oysters and amber spiked bon-bons in small goblets
on the cemetery gravestones.

I will pick my nose in company, and I will play the fiddle.

When I die, the gnome and the elf from Norway will make me
into small leather shoes and little leather aprons for the
children of a nearby mushroom dealer.

OBSIDIAN MOON

At sunrise I meet a woman
      spying on spiders, lichen, and larks.
She grows fangs and a witch's tit.
      Birds delight in her ecstatic clamor.

At twilight I meet a kerchiefed woman
      leading three children by the hands:
one white rabbit, one black papaya seed,
      one flesh-red pipestone.

All over this planet
      certain ones join me,
in silence, in slow motion—
      appear inside me,
the way breath whitens inside crystal glass.

I grow old and thin
      as the moon does
when it turns toward the shadows
      of itself.

When I have welcomed each stranger,
      men will look up
to obsidian moon,
      ripe, dark, and true.

FROM A YELLOW SQUASH WOMAN

I wake this morning
smoothing my full yellow squash breasts
and thighs with my hands.

If I love him,
which I will decide any minute,
I will follow him anywhere,
even out of the wet ground
where I grow in sweet gold fits and starts.

FOR A YOUNG SOUTH DAKOTA MAN

I no longer want to meet
people who have no muscles.

I love your muscles.
I love the barbwire cuts in your
    tan-gold shoulder,
the rattlesnake skin tied around
    your head,
the way your hands curl like warm rabbits
    beside the campfire.

I planted a lilybulb,
hoed the corn,
rode the horse,
swam in muddy Missouri,
toed a dusty toad
with you
    green green green green
        you.

I'm in love with the way
the land loves you,
the way you greet
    morning wildrose
    afternoon fence post
    evening fire under forest leaves.

You show me how to walk
in the country dark:
    Black soil in waves
    under white moon Dakota.
    Black soil seep,
    sing Dakota.
    Black soil in your fingernails,
    white sweat on your forehead.

You speak of farmlights,
and the north forty.
You speak of choosing a home
by swimming toward it through river water at night
and judging whether you need to live there
by listening to the animal sounds on shore.

You move with light in you
toward me in the dark.
When you open your mouth and eyes,
light rides out of you toward me.

I no longer want to meet
people who have swallowed no living light from black soil.

BILLY AND BONES

Bones. Bones is dead.
He had black hair.
Sang a song called, "Long Black Veil."
Ribs in his chest
thrummed
like a harp
in an undercurrent.
"Oh la la la, Oh la la la la."

Bones made love to me last night
under a hollow tree
with wet lips and teeth
and plump thumbs.
He rose above me
like a hungry tornado.
I lay back in the rain,
my hair falling
like shagbark
behind me.

Once, Bones, when you lived,
I heard you
make love to your bone self
in the next bed.
I sweated.
I had a meek hope.

Bones,
Billy is alive.
He made love to me
inside an egg.
He has a pony tail
and teeth that can cut lips.
He is gone to California
in a red flash.
I want him here.

Bones,
go get Billy.
Tell him to come here.
Send him to me wrapped in a scarf.
Tell him to love me
with wonder at the wrinkles on my wrists and neck
where the sun locks me into the world
beside black water
where Bones
sleeps and rubs and spirals
away.

MALE POETS

My mother
knows
about poets.
"Oh these poets,"
she says.
"Keep away from them."
Gawking through doors and windows,
they call the turkey a phoenix,
call the mashed potatoes Mountains of Myrrh,
call me Sappho.
They become murderers, rapists,
or shoe salesmen
at will,
or, god help us,
horses,
or the ghosts of horses.
They travel long distance
to write odes to each other
at the ocean
without touching water or foam,
until the following Saturday
when they bring a cup of cool beer
to their lips.
And what would one
make of me
in bed? padding
my good lines,
editing my best lines,
fiercely counting
my feet?

I HATE YOU, YOU MAN

What in the world
did you mean
when the smoke in your mouth
filled the tunnel of my throat?

What did you think
when you lifted me, kiss,
and turned me, kiss,
and mashed me playfully,
and followed one of my blue veins
through my body
to my heart
with your finger?

I tell you, man,
I was there.
Like the ham bone in the paper bag,
like the rock near your eye,
like the sand flea on your wrist
were there.

YOU CAN GET MEN AT THE GENERAL STORE

I visit a trailer park
in California.
Day after day I smoke
with widows, college girls, waitresses
waiting under clotheslines.

A woman of 52 with a blond ponytail
says men are no problem
to get anymore
if you want them.
"At the General Store," she says,
pointing an arrow finger.

I go to the general store;
down Aisle 3
a low growl
directs me to the Sex Dept.

In a huge showroom
men wearing leisure suits and space helmets
are strapped to platforms on the ceiling.
Each woman customer chooses
which pink, violet, or red floor platform
she wants to lie down on.
The attendant pushes the correct lever.
Ceiling and floor
glide together in space.

I choose violet. I lie back.
The man in the space helmet descends
as I rise.
Closer, his eyes are blue.
He might be an old friend working part-time for cash.
Closer, his eyes are lovely.
He might be Bill.

I will make my eyes lovely.
I will make him love me more
than the other women at the General Store.

A NEW WAY OF WALKING

Today my silk body
moves
like one ripple apart from the stream,
like silver-wet
fish muscle
in the sun.

I am so delicate.
The flower I took from the man underwater
coils in the clear marrow of my eyes.

His hands
and the hair on his hands
tickled me deftly
all night.
I am
vulnerable
vein by vein
to a man with breath
coming from his pores.

He put his hand
into me
and pulled out
this fountain
this rare smell of a water drop.

LAKE NUBANUSIT, NEW HAMPSHIRE

I swim from shore alone.
I look back toward three men on the sand.

Water laps at my lower lip.
A water drop on one eyelash
is as large as the head of one of the men.

They are lounging
and sucking beer
and roaring with laughter
about a breast joke.
One watches me,
another kicks up his heels,
a third tilts his throat to the sun.

I hang
in green.
I look down.
My dim hands
tend my body.
I finger the scratch on my outer thigh
and the stretch marks on my inner thigh.
I press my swollen breasts bobbing.
I lace my fingers in my toes.

I am a water animal
on watch in the weeds of my hair.
I am a fish and they have poles.
I am a web foot.
They are tooth and nail.
I am the frog's throat bulge.
They are the prongs of stars.

I love them.
They would save me from drowning and
they think I am beautiful.
I heard them say so
across the water
with the huge cones
of my coral ears.

The salmon-colored flowers of my body open
and tremble
in the lake water.

THE LONELINESS OF THE LOVERS

When I meet you,
I am aroused and excited.
I buzz and tingle and drink gold beer.

I want to embrace you.
I am exalted. I fill with echoes.
I reel and fall in coils across your lap.

Soon,
I want to become you.
"I *am* Heathcliff," I warble.

One morning
you walk into me and say, puzzled, to yourself,
"What's going on?
Where am I?
I was here a minute ago."

Meanwhile I lurch around the room.
"Where is he?
Where'd he go?
He was here a minute ago."

"Oh there you are," I shout,
as you appear suddenly.
"Where were you?"

"I don't know," you say, scratching your head.
"But let's not do that again."

WHAT DO YOU WANT TO DO ON SATURDAY?

The same thing I want to do
every day.

I want to eat Henry
under the burning bush
with an arrow in my heart,
an arrow of love.

I want to lick Henry,
lick his circled eyes
with my hands tied in his hair
and my laugh, laugh, laugh.

I want to stand
ten feet away from Henry
and draw pictures of him on my thighs
with a cigar-shaped stone.

I want to drink clear gin with Henry
in the clear stream,
break open the raw fish he catches,
prick my fingers on the bone.

I want to marry Henry,
even his wife and his child,
and take them all with me
into my heart, my house that drowns.

FIVE PRAISE POEMS FOR A MARRIED MAN

I

Let's parade down Main Street,
wear embroidery and feathers,
throw clover and crackerjacks,
and shout, "Hurrah!"

Find a big yellow duck to strut downtown behind him,
because he has a sweet grin.
Find him a steady pattern of rain on a cabin roof
because he has kind eyes.
Find him a music box
because he has playful fingers and wavy hair.
Find him a vial of mist
because of his whimsical way of walking around grocery stores.

Give him a fortune cookie with almonds. Give him a red
bird-berry. Give him a hug and a whole lot of delicate pinches.

I have discovered a mantra in him, a mother who loved,
a mimosa blossom, a man on horseback, a many-splendored thing.

He is more stalwart than Babe Ruth at bat,
smoother than Wilt the Stilt blocking shots,
more beautiful than Monroe's body in blue water,
> more painful to me
> than sand in the heart valve
> or my first grey hair.

II

Why don't I
have the steady company
of a man like this?

Was I in the next phone booth talking to Auntie Ellen
in 1962 when he needed a dime?
Was I musing into red wine in 1964
when he sat across from me and ordered beer?
Was I reading the Want Ads in 1968
when he tried to catch my eye?
Did I leave my matches at home in 1970
the day he needed a light?

Or is my hair too bright and tangled?
(I should get it frosted and netted.)
Is my walk too much a stride?
(I should wear high heels and walk with buttoned buttocks.)
Does my face remind people of baked bread and cream
on the corn cob?
(I should wear purple eye-shadow and red dresses with slits.)

Or am I reluctant
to walk head-on
toward any unmarried man?

III

Men are dangerous.
They might ignite or explode when goaded.
They might balance on tightropes, climb cliffs,
fall off while they show off.
They might join the army
or the army might join them.
They might take up a lot of space,
complain about overcrowding,
eat most of the food.
They might declare themselves ruler,
or owner, or emperor of something.
They might not think they are funny.
They might not know that I matter.

IV

My sister is more sympathetic.
She can put up with cheap blackberry brandy,
small infidelities,
tag-around buddies,
piano music and fist fights at 3 a.m.
She can put up with week-after-lackadaisical-week,
and dead silence on the other end of the phone
when she is angry.
She can put up with black balloons on the sunporch,
elephant toe-muck on the pillow,
pimples in the cracks
and no whispering.
     I can't.
     Things are bad enough as I am
     for heaven sake.

V

It occurs to me
I may live alone all my life
inside some house I find, pay for, keep clean,
and invite guests to,
while this lovely married parade man
sleeps with another woman called "wife"
in their space called "home"
every
single
night.

Any solutions?

One. Kill myself. Slash my wrists to shreds to flakes
   to ashes.

Two. Dance with him.
   Hold him in my arms
   when he's not there
   because he's thinking about his wife,
   though he did ask me to dance.

Three. Count money into boxes. Arrange folds in curtains.
   Scold squirrels.

Four. Become independent of all this by moving to Nova
   Scotia and changing my name and the names of all
   the things I do:

   I'll call "kissing," "blueberrying,"
   and I'll call "beer-drinking," "loon-hungering,"
   and I'll call "discussing Martin Buber,"
   "lurching under fodder."

   And my name will be:

   everforever, una, amen, fortuna, happy hooker,
   cockleshell, makepeace thackeray Manfred.

THE EVIL THINGS I THINK ABOUT MEN AND DO NOT SAY

He might
stay awake all night
and flick away my dreams
with his hand.

How does he know
I'm not dreaming to become
a fat snake or a blue eel?

I admit
I smashed an eel once
flat as a pancake.
Rolled it up and smoked it.

I imagine him soft,
an overbaked Cornish hen,
shrinking into my stomach
whenever I need him.

I pull him out,
cradle him,
diddle him on my knee,
feed mashed beets into his toothless mouth.

You will never know the most evil thing I think about men.

I hope their whole body falls off.

SAM'S BALLS

Alls
I know
is
Sam's balls
hang out of his new underwear
but I never notice.

WHY I HATE (AND WONDER ABOUT) THESE POETRY READINGS

One time at my poetry reading in Mission, South Dakota,
a very angular blond person with a neck brace holding up his chin
fell on the floor laughing hard during one of my more serious
lyrical poems.

During my reading in Palo Alto, California, a man named Elroy,
who sat in the back row, decided I was basically a man instead
of a woman. Afterwards he took me out for a drink at the
Black Spider Bar. I was lighting a candle with a match when
he noticed I was a woman, twice blessed, and he tossed his drink
against the velvet wall, jumped into his Volkswagen, and buzzed
off.

The day after I gave a poetry reading at Boulder, Colorado, a man
wearing a raincoat came to my front door holding a cake of soap
and a blue towel. He asked if he could use my shower.
"What?" I said.
"I heard you mention you had one," he said.

At a reading in Beaver Creek, Minnesota, a 98 year old lady
named Adeline Jenny waved at me from the front row the whole
time. When I finished she rolled her wheelchair over, gave me
a yeasty kiss, and said, "Come and visit me sometime! Now I've
got glasses my brains are bran new." And she added, beaming
and patting my hand, "I couldn't hear a word you said up there."

After a reading at an Indian boarding school in South Dakota,
I ate greasy bologna, lettuce with milk-dressing, and pulpy
white bread in a dungeon lunchroom with three kids on detention.
One kid told me he was partly bald on top because the principal
kept pulling the hairs out of his head one by one. He hated
poems, he told me. They reminded him of mouse squeaks.

Another time a freckled girl wearing an evening gown with sweat moons under the armpits told me my poems made her realize her deep hatred for her husband, the doctor. She said she was dying for me to help her get rid of him so she could become a rock musician.

After reading love poems at The MacDowell Colony in August, I heard a knock on my door in the black night. A man with a blackberry in his mouth opened the door and beckoned for me to kiss him. When I didn't, he threw some ferns on my piano and left.

There are more reasons why I wonder about poetry readings:

In San Francisco I read for Educational Television, and when they showed the program, my head was on from right to left instead of left to right. I was beside myself because I looked older and more foolish than I remembered.

From the tape of a radio performance in Los Gatos, California, they removed my voice and substituted a new born baby warbling my words.

In Ithaca, New York, a man who was too handsome sat during my entire hour performance eyeing a girl across the aisle, making pear-shaped gestures toward her with his left hand. He had huge dimples in his brown cheeks and I could see my poems dripping word by word into them.

Also in Ithaca a lady in the front row yawned ten times and sighed twice as loud as a hog. She looked at her watch six times, fingered her big toe through the hole in her moccasin, chewed gum, and glared at me.

So, who am I
that I should keep you
from your breathing,
your kissing,
your raving,
and your sizzling bacon
and ask you to listen to my poems?

I'm too sinewy.
I lunge.
I fall down.
I talk out of my bellybutton from under my hat.
The tongue curl of my heart unwinds and flaps and flaps and flaps.

I suggest you go get a drink
or a cup of coffee.
I can't bear your attention.
I am askew on this perch.

Go talk to yourself in your natural voice.

THE DOG IN THE BAR-ROOM MIRROR

Unexpectedly a mirror reveals me
as I am, a country hick, pure ham
and potato spuds and beer. Unabashed
the toothy grin stands forth, and
the large breasted body and the childish chin.
Compose yourself, I say, this is not
the best day on record as the Almanac (Farmer's)
and the faces at the bar have said. Joy is dead.
But beside me in the mirror a friendly dog
steps forth, rollicking the tiled floor,
nearly unhinging the door with glee. Flapping
ears hang free. This is me?
Restrict that giggle, you. There's no
room for a wiggler in your booth. It's uncouth.
Go back to where you sit with teachers
drear and fat debating in their drink.
I turn to go, but first I bend
to give myself a quick, consoling pat.

MY BASKETBALL BROTHER VERSUS WINDOM

Nine players
shuttled down the floor,
red and white, blue and gold,
leaving the tenth,
my brother Fred, red and white,
politely grasping his stomach
above the groin
where Miller No. 31
had elbowed him in the balls.

My brother fell
on his back,
groaned and twitched
for five minutes.

My father
stood up straight nearly seven feet tall
and shouted,
"Number 31 is a killer, goddamit!"
My mother asked,
"What did Number 31 do that for?
D'you think he meant to hit Fred?"
I put one hand over my mouth
and chanted, "Oh Freddy, oh Freddy,"
(as if he weren't 18 years old)
and groaned
because part of my body
that will never be part of my body
was hurt.

The referee
asked my brother not to swear,
AND he called the original foul
on my brother.

My father leaped seven feet
straight into the air
and said, "What?!?"
so loud
that six women sitting in front of us
exchanged wigs
and turned into hunchbacks.

We tried to jerk my father down
        out of the air
where he was floating
in a black cloud.
Everyone stared at mother and me
        as if we had
brought an Alaskan black bear
into the gym
without a chain.

My heart
kept leaving my chest
and going up for a rebound in my throat.
I called the referee OUT
on 40 technicals.
I pulled his black stripes
way out from his back
and let them snap back into the white stripes.

I did not enjoy the rest of the game.
Behind the prancing cheerleaders,
who pretended not to know about
their wide-split legs,
I saw monsters,
growing from human organs,
wounding and lashing
in the small town gym.

The sweetest thing of the night
was my own sweet brother
and his beautiful body
getting up off the floor
with all his blood inside.

GRANDMA SHORBA AND THE PURE IN HEART

My mother's mother's underpants
made me not want to grow up.
And my belief that she kept an ax
in the top of her old-fashioned chain toilet
convinced me I wouldn't live that long anyway.
          She used to sneak into the bathroom
at midnight for the ax
and search to kill me,
because she knew I suspected
she was secretly a murderer.
          She saw me notice
the thin warts, like rice grains,
growing on end out of her neck.
She saw me stare at her long floppy breasts
and the pink, wide-legged underpants
falling off her hips.
The crotch hung down like a handle,
not broad enough to hide
mouse-nest pubic hair,
less grey than her head hair.
          I was so glad I had skinny underpants
and an eel's rear end,
glad I did not have to stir tired bones
to make tea for visitors all day,
or feed the men who begged quarters, bread, and wine
at the pantry door.
          I figured she used that ax at night
after giving in all day
to people who took advantage.
          She was so NICE.
She had to have something else going for her.

Grandmothers
have caused me a lot of trouble and pity.
        Like my great-grandmother in Iowa.
She died. But somehow when we drove back to Minnesota
after the funeral, she was lying in the oblong space
between the front and back seat of my dad's Ford.
In the front seat Dad and Uncle Floyd teased each other
about the correct grip for newfangled steering wheels,
their faces alight in the glow of speedometer, clock,
and gas gauges.
        I was curled into a ball
in the dark caverns of the back seat.
Smack between me and the joke-cracking men lay my
dead great-grandmother, who wanted to snatch me,
because I ate four ham sandwiches and the whole plate
of mints at her funeral, despite the heavy smell of rotton
gums and perfumed moth balls.
        Lucky Dad was around, because she glared,
fierce and very positive about something,
her eyes like live coals on the floor of the car,
        so completely dead when I wasn't.

My worst "grandmother" was May Belle Harmer,
my day care nurse, a "lovely woman," who loved me
"very much," mother said.
But May Belle would not let me straddle the toilet
and pee facing the wall like Dad.
"Teeny gals harn't made that way."
        I wanted to be like Dad,
glancing amiably out the window at the pine trees,
staring at the fly specks on the wall,
casual and leisurely,
        NOT facing front,
committed to a seat, staring at May Belle's slitty eyes,
pursed lips, stomach like a cow (and gurgling like a cow too).
"Face front!" she'd shout.

Under my breath she was Old Mad Hatter or March Hare.
    As soon as she left,
I swiveled and faced the wall.
Then I could relax, lean my elbows on the flat top
of the toilet tank, like at a Woolworth's lunch counter,
and pour myself lemon sodas from Mother's powder box.

May Belle didn't trust Woolworth's lunch counters
because of the germs drunk people left on the salt and pepper.
When she saw a drunk man in the street,
she shriveled up her jowls and ushered me away.
        I preferred going out
with my mother's mother, Grandma Shorba
(of the underpants) and talking with the drunk men.
No sooner did we spot a White Castle than we'd be
at the counter for a treat. I could order six Castleburgers
without a struggle from Grandma Shorba, and eat them
on the bus home.
        And at home she had Easter Eggs,
cream-filled chocolates, caraway soup with dumplings
and cucumbers with cream. During dinner I sang,
    "Dog, dog, sing a happy sog."
Grandma shouted, "Song, song, you silly goose, not *sog*.
There's no such word."
        Both giggling, because the business
of fitting rhyme to meaning could go too far,
and make you sober as a judge.

After dinner Grandma Shorba went to church
to hear Missionary Fern and her husband, Billy Jean.
        If her legs ached, she stayed home
and read the obituaries, of people she knew and people
she didn't know, to me.
        She finished with accounts of auto accidents,
about mangled blond girls with severed heads,
broken hearts, and tortured legs, in some drunken
highway pile-up.

"Lord have mercy,"
twitching the paper and her cheeks, hitching up her eyeglasses.
She showed me a photograph
of her only son, George,
who died in a motorcycle-car accident when he was fifteen.
George had one arm draped over the silver-
studded saddle, one leg cocked on the cycle runner. Grandma
had hung a red-padded cloth heart over the corner of the
photograph, which I still see
as clearly as the thumbprints I left
on the carefully shined glass.
"George was young and proud and beautiful,"
Grandma said. "He begged me for a birthday motorcycle. God
forgive me, I bought it for him." She showed me where she had
written in a diary:
It is God's will
that He did not want George to suffer here.
He was too sweet and good,
and called home long before his allotted time.
Since that time I have not lived,
waiting for that meeting day in my Father's
house, as He has promised.
On the bottom of the page she added:
The Pure In Heart shall see God.
No one in this life could take Georgie's place.

A few years before George was born, Grandma herself was
startled and run over by a speeding car. She said she
broke all the bones in her body except two. She pulled
her skirt up to show me a purple crescent-shaped gouge
on the inside of her knee.
I stared at the puckered skin grafts
and told her it looked like a horse had stomped her with one
hoof. She said it felt like 100 hooves.
After hearing the obituaries
and chanting "Jesus Loves Me" with Grandma,

I crawled into bed and lay awake
with my back against Grandma's warm back. She snored,
vibrating steadily against me. I rubbed the delicate skin
of my wrists back and forth over the hairy sheets Grandma
bought in basement sales.
    I pictured Grandma being run over, stomped,
and the shiver of her bones, and the slivers.
I summoned the flash of her hidden ax in the toilet top,
        sharp for her next
        retaliatory midnight outing.

It was amazing how Grandma forgot where she put everything,
so when we went to the movies we were always late.
        "It's just that I've had so much trouble,"
        she said, "in life."
That's why her glasses were in the silverware tray
and why her gloves were not beside her hat.
Dear Jesus usually helped her find them,
        though I kept a sharp eye out myself.
Sometimes I got so mad looking for Grandma's hat pin,
that I pinched her arms and the rolls of fat at her waist
all the way to the movies, shrieking like a harpy,
leaping away from the slaps of her fingers.
        "Stop that!" she said.
        "Now keep still. Keep still."
"I won't. I'll talk all during this dumb movie."
        "You keep still."
"You owe me two dollars for candy, Grandma," I concluded.
        "Hussst! You keep still,
        and I'll tell you a good parrot story:
In a cold attic in the Old Country two blue-lipped
servant girls worked for a bare living.
Their rich mistress wore a gorgeous green wool dress
and a gold locket. She owned a fat green parrot
who croaked, 'Polly wants! Polly wants!' at the
servant girls, while they stayed up all night
sewing fancy new dresses for the lady.

The girls got mad"
(Grandma's lips twitched and she got a gleam in her eye.)
        "so one night
    they stitched up the parrot's hind end with a green
    thread. The lady kept feeding her parrot until it died."
I squirmed for the world's dumb animals when Grandma concluded:
    "The parrot couldn't tell the lady its problem."

We still weren't at the movies, because Grandma
walked slowly with her badly mended legs.
I kept dancing ahead into the darkest shadows,
        so she told me another story
about a man, crippled worse than she was after her car accident,
who got trapped in midstreet by an oncoming trolly.
        He lay down to pray
between two trolly tracks, and got up untouched when the car
passed over him. (Dear Jesus again.)

Grandma said Jesus could see around corners,
so I kept him for my friend when I went out alone
in the woods or the high swamp grass.
        Grandma said
Jesus loved little girls like me,
but he shouldn't take me away like he took George.
        "Why did he take George, Grandma?"
"Because he was always too good for this world,
my own precious boy,
        God forgive me."

God forgive you?
Dear Grandma, please, before I get old
or run over by a car, I forgive you.
Do you forgive me?
        I forgive everything,
even the image of your underpants,
that makes me quake with laughter this morning
and reach down to touch my unprotected self.

I'm going to sew
a padded red heart
for my own true dead love's photograph,
and make care-away soup
for my own boy or girl.
And I don't expect you
to come back from the grave
into my house or my car at midnight
            with an ax or anything.
I understand
you're much happier there with Jesus.

Jesus would still be with me too,
but I found a horse named Chita Maria.
            If it hadn't been for you
            I wouldn't have owned that horse.
You couldn't stand to hear me cry
young honey tears all night,
so you gave Dad money for Chita Maria
and a silver-studded saddle.
            It's a good thing, Grandma.
That horse was the first dancing friend
I loved so much I could have died.
I grew up
so I could ride her alone
across the Minnesota River.

            I hope you are doing well
            with George and the flying ghosts
            in your Father's house
            where you belong,
            you sweet, you startled woman,
            you burdened heart
            of my heart.

THERE IS SOMETHING WORSE

There is something worse
than fear of incest with the father, or the mother:
    it is the dread
of your mother's friend, the one
who stands at your mother's left in your dreams,
    whose body
has the same contour as all human bodies,
but no memorable features.
The face is blank.
The hands do not move.

This friend of your mother's
never speaks to anyone except your mother.
Your mother does not want her to speak
with the red-cheeked grandmother skittering over the ice,
who greets you with passion and approval.
Nor may she speak with the frost-bearded old man by the
        bonfire,
or the other skaters, or the sparrows picking
bread crumbs off the ice.

Your mother's friend speaks to no one:
and the only way you know she has a voice
is because your mother's lips move
when the two face each other;
and the only way you know
her body is solid
is when a sparrow tries to fly through her
and falls back, stunned, on the ice.
        And the reason you can't meet her
must be because your mother is
desperately attracted
to her unfinished condition.

You stand on the ice and watch your mother
and her best friend for a long time,
wishing to join them,
but permanently uninvited. You become aware
that your coat, your hat and your boots
are missing. You are very cold;
you cannot walk home without the boots:
and the unfashionable black ice skates
with the sharp silver blades
which you borrowed from the boy next door
will not hold you up
much longer.

POEM TO MY SISTER

I

You look like
the long-haired blond woman
in my nightmare
who says she will kill.
I am trying to be a strong woman,
trying to sleep
and cover my scars.

Blond woman looks like me,
only cleaner, whiter, blonder,
newer,
and despite those, wiser.
She is one perfect
danger.

II

I have noticed
the sweet white bread rising in your body, sister,
in your breasts and around your hips.

I hear a blond silk hum, high and pure,
in your hair, your fingernails,
and in the short hair around your lips.

You seem so certain when you go to sleep
that you are doing the best thing for that hour
by folding away your green stockings.

III

While you sleep
you drool, chanting,
"No, mother; mother, no,
nomo, onmo, mono, omno."

You wake with fear.
Father bears down, a thunder cloud
flashing lightning.
I arrive soon after, a brief hard rain.

It is amazing your sun
creeps out afterward.
You create fur boxes, glass bananas,
dolls in treasure chests.

IV

My heart just jumped twice
out of rhythm
because I remember how you stood in the clear
pine night with the man I loved,
whose poems made me cry.
You were holding him
in your white arms,
perfect as moon bones,
swallowing him
with wild cream-and-blue eyes.
    And you wrote in your notes to yourself,
    "Sister, I'm sorry."

No place for me to take my body,
swollen like a bladder,
lips like rubber,
numb throat muscles.
No wonder I couldn't sing.

That's where you live most, sister,
in your wise and woman throat,
where all your beauty pours out complete.
Singing!
The goat, the peacock and the dog listen on the hill.
Men put down their drinks.
The wind rewinds.

See, this is how I feel,
in my bloated sorrow,
my snake anger,
love under my lifted eyebrows,
in my kind eyes.

Do not touch your silver hands
to the wounds of my best man,
and I will let flowers grow forever
out of my throat
when I see you.

THE DREAM I SAY I DON'T UNDERSTAND

This poem is for my lover, who wants to be a giant
octopus, growing tentacles through the sea in eight
sacred directions. He desires the dread water mother
who gave birth to him—cheek to jowl with otter,
holy ghost of oyster, and the frog who tends the stream
of childhood.

I have a dream,
ripe seed,
that splits my soul
as child,
as girl,
and now, as woman.

Dream of a young boy
living in a boathouse
by the sea.
He wears white trousers
with pale blue cuffs.
Muscles ripple in his back
like the wings of birds
under water.

He walks in a green garden,
in a feathery sage,
bay leaf,
caraway, cassia
garden.
He watches the water,
the leaps of the water,
the blur, the caress,
the beautiful water,
the water that cares.

His eyes reflect
crescents of light
that flash off the water.
He looks like me
and like Jesus Christ,
with wavy red hair,
long fingers,
sparks showering into water
throughout his body.

I live in a mansion on the hill
with old people.
I sneak down to see this boy every evening.
They could never imagine
how we talk on the stone wall,
how we smile
and mingle and move.
We have been born knowing
they would forbid us each other.

One night Grandmother Moon
and her lover, Grandfather Dust,
hover above me
in a brown rocking chair
shiny with oil.
Grandmother Moon
twines her hair around her lower lip,
which is sexy and red and puffy
for one so old,
and tells me
the boy is really my brother.

She says he was crazy when he was born.
Grey marl and grape leaves
twisted on his head,
so they hid him in the boathouse.
They regretted his soft arms
and lovely face
and hated him for his beauty.

When Grandmother Moon
tells me I can't be with him,
I rise, put my thumb in my mouth
and bite it off.
I weep straight into the river.
I scream until my lungs fold
back to gills.
No one hears.

I run to the garden.
Glow worms twiggle in the bushes.
He is already running to me
when he sees me.
His arms snag me.
Warm, warm.

I am afraid to grow up
and lose him.
His gorgeous head
grows out of the center
of the wild rose.
He is my passion.
What will happen?

WINTER DREAM

My sister runs over the snow,
with sweeping yellow hair.
Her eyes burn like rubies.
She takes my hand in her own.

We strain toward the far field
that lifts to the blizzard's whip.
My red hair flames like embers,
stirred by ice and wind.

My eyes are gold, like a new pear.
My lips like a pear curve, too.
I've long legs, distant legs, white,
and a whirlpool where they meet.

We find you curled on a high ridge,
with lamb's wool and antelope horn,
beneath your feet a bundle,
the bones of your mother, well-wrapped.

Your face waxes young with sleep, man,
and your face wanes old with dreams.
Cold bites deep at your skull.
Your mouth is frozen wide.

Sister-with-soft-hands stays with you,
while I run home to get fuel.
Cornrows long and cornstalks bent
point the road to the cave.

And now I enter the cave, man,
where you stand at my sister's side,
both of you warm at the hearth,
new blood live in your cheeks.

The goblet in your hand, man,
has a thin stem, finger bone.
The wine inside turns to blood,
drops to the stone-hearth bed.

My heart closes tight as a fist.
My heart opens boldly — a rose.
It's fist over heart over fist, man,
till the snow buries dreams like this.

FAMILY FALLING APART

My sister,
curled in bed
with jelly bones,
watches transparent snakes
crawl toward her.

My brother
stiffens his cheek muscles,
cracks his knuckles.
He has never hurt us.
His bones are still growing.

I smile a gash
and turn my head backward
to get through the house.
My bones are trying to
get out of my mouth through my throat.

Mother's eyes,
peeled grapes,
say she has no excuse.
She stands, lost,
next to the refrigerator.
She can't find her way
from the toaster to the breadbox.

Father's eyes
don't see us.
Lucky for him, he has a dream house
up in a tree
where he keeps a surprise box of raisins,
and eats them,
one by one,
sweet titmouse raisins,
by himself.

Oh my family
stay in the cave inside me.
You aren't ready to be born.

Super nova father,
planet mother,
far far sister star,
exploding brother star,
how will I touch you?
in all this empty breathing out,
breathing out,
breathing out.

ALICE'S POEM

I never met Grandma Alice.
Dad said she was six-foot
        and wouldn't hurt a fly.
She was Dad's dead mother
        so he told me
all about how she was saint-like
        and a wet smoocher.
She smelled like butter,
and milk, and steam.
Her breasts were full and white,
her eyes as blue as her garden bluebells.
She brought her face down
to their thin bluebell mouths,
linking herself to their suckling roots.
She knelt in the soil to urge
roses up trellises, plant lettuce, weed peas.
        But the more Dad described,
the less I wanted to be her double.

She spoke a gentle language, "Shoot,"
        when her mother meddled in pots and pans,
when five sons' record fly balls
shattered the porch windows:
        "Fred's fault!" cried Floyd.
        "No, Ed's!" vowed John, as
        little Aben cheered,
        husband Frank chuckled,
        and Henry-to-be kicked inside
        his warm Alice stomach.
"Shoot!" said Alice. "Oh shoot."

She enveloped her seven men with farm food:
brown loaves, chokecherry jelly,
abounding egg-cheese.
    And God enveloped her: erect in a pew,
she glowed in the colors that flowed
through the church windows with the sun's rays.
    When there was no church, she'd play
the organ by herself in the parlor,
and pause, after "Beautiful Ohio,"
      to watch green cottonwood leaves
      flip white
in the early morning breeze.

On Alice's red lips was a white dust,
as from a moth's wing.
She was born with heart walls
thin as bluebell petals.
Though the rest of her body grew
older and wiry, her heart fluttered—
fine as the placenta
around a new-born calf.
    She had a hole in her heart,
through which breath escaped her,
through which death came
slender as the early morning breeze,
when she was thirty-eight.
    Farmwife Alice,
the only woman in a house full of men,
first dead.
    Her young husband buried her
and sat up till dawn
wondering how to grow a baby and five boys
without their muse.
    . . .

Alice's wedding photo showed a crown of red hair
and freckles, like mine, Dad said.
      Everyone who was older than sixteen
said I would grow up to be like Alice:
standing straight as a cornstalk in a white lace dress,
encircled by an arm in a black suit,
the paler color of a pair,
behind me, in shadow, a solid male body,
with a face as intent as a winter's day.
      Nope, I said (when I was ten).
      I'll live in a stormy woodland
      where I'll lick rain from bushes,
            eat raw meat, and wear cowboy boots.
      I'll fish the streams,
            mounted on a snapping turtle.
I didn't want to grow up and become
too gentle for words, with an eaten-away heart.

I wanted to be a fighter like Dad
in the T.B. sanitarium, on his back
for two years, watching white sheets
grow higher and higher up his chest
like a frostline in October.
      He refused hospital food, "Pap!"—
scared the white-capped waves of nurses
into bringing armloads of farm eggs, greens,
and news of weather in the haying fields.
He couldn't let his lungs be eaten,
like Alice's heart.
      When Dad described T.B.
his long arms tensed
so the silver-blue veins stood out,
his fists clenched
as if he could drive them into solid rock
and awaken silence.
      I looked for friends
tough and two-fisted enough to get me through,
after talking with Dad about "licking T.B."
and hearts with holes born right in them.
                  . . .

My first friend was Eugene V. Debs, a golden retriever,
who galloped with me into fields of yellow mustard,
licked my lips until blood rose.
　　He defended me against cosmetic salesmen and
insurance investigators, and I fell in love
with slurping dog assaults; but Debs was sold.
He sat on top of me too long, in his virile way:
　　"He was a hunter at heart," Dad said.
I wanted to be a hunter too, since I
shouldn't be the prey.
　　　　　　　. . .

My next friend was a mustang,
brown, with a black stripe down her back,
who clicked her teeth at bare arms
and bugled through her nostrils on winter nights.
She bled each month, and flirted her eyelashes
at the stallions in the meadow.
She hunted the wind in four directions
whenever she pleased.
　　She was bred, and gave birth to twins,
and they died, wrapped in their placentas,
with unformed hooves.
　　　　　　　. . .

My animal friends
rated more than human.
They had room to breathe with free lungs,
and red hearts always pounding strong.
They roamed, played, and bred
with claws and snarls, and humped
the neighbor's species as their own.
They were like nothing
you could find gentle language for;
and yet they died, or left,
or carried death inside them
to my door.

These worries belong to Dad.
He's Alice's first son. He needs her as often
as he says I'm just like her.
But I am the first woman
born after all those men who didn't die;
and Alice knows her mark on me.

Listen, Alice, you tell me
the bloody secrets Dad couldn't inherit:
        Did you ever run, raging,
down those long corn rows?
        Who did you threaten, as you
bled six boys?
        Please, what did you keep
for yourself—except the concave grave?
        If you tell me these secrets,
I'll let go of mine:

        There's a lake in the woods
        I visit often in my dreams.
        A stream, flowing from the hinterlands,
        pours into the lake,
        and I always track it back,
        bend after bend.
        It's the only stream on earth
        that grows deeper and wider
        toward its source.

And last night you were at the lake, Alice,
and I asked you to go with me
up the last half of the stream
        where I hadn't dared to go
        in thirty years of dreams.
You wouldn't do it, Alice, and it
wasn't because you didn't love me enough,
and yet it WAS.
        It's our secret, but my stream, Alice.
So I'll go with you, sweet and gentle,
        the first half—
and go alone,
        aroused and fierce, the second.

                    . . .

My second secret is a story, Alice:

        I was born a twin, along with a boy,
                a hunter,
        with fists and a dog's long tongue.

        I've been lonely since my twin died.
        In dreams he died and died and died
        inside me, a boy who was afraid of women,
        because women have such delicate hearts.

        When my twin was alive
                I couldn't love.
        I couldn't die.
        I couldn't bequeath absences.

He died, this boy inside,
so I can be
as woman as a heart
like the petals of a bluebell—
as woman as the animal heart
crouched primitive, in me.

WEDDING SONG

I will

live with you
blessed
with reason
and rhyme.

Say with you
worlds unsaid;
pray with you
for plain words.

Strong of eye,
cry with you;
happy mouth
laugh.

Fire upon flame
rage with you,
may blue rain
follow.

Wing over wing
wrap you
to my breast
at evening.

Sigh over sigh
match the wind
in absent
presence.

Wish for wish
wake you,
want for want
take you.

Try for try
push on ahead,
following your ghost
into the wilderness.

Old song after old song,
I'll sing for new weather—
sing of new shapes
for unchanging love.

THE WOMAN IN THE ASPEN GROVE

I lie awake with the wind
at the end of summer.
      Before daybreak
a woman floats from my body,
and walks down a corridor of trees
toward the aspen grove
at the end of the lane.

I hurry from bed to the window.
Rising from the grove's hollow
I hear a voice, just born,
trill and water fall.
She sings what I learned inside my mother
and forgot before my birth:

> "The hollow black pupils of your eyes
> bloom toward the face of your lover,
> blacker, and more vast,
> as love ripens.
>
> The door doesn't give;
> the space where the door was, takes.
> The ocean doesn't close upon the shore;
> the shore, near and far, opens,
> like the O that opens in your mouth
> when you die.
>
> Rise up too early in the morning,
> without dreams or lovers to hold you,
> and watch the dark let go:
> walls disgorge windows,
> black sacs turn inside out, spewing light.
> See how open dark is—
> and how light believes in it."

Emptiness rises inside me—
like the absence of an unloving mother
growing through childhood
and opening, to swallow an adult.

The emptiness
grows gorgeous, blooms
in my throat.
I open the window

to scream my first word.

AMERICAN ROADS

I

In spring
    snow geese going north
clatter on the slough.
    I'm off
along the road
again.

Lean back,
    let go.
Hwy 90 slithers west,
    snaps into 29.

        Two giants sit in two oceans
        and grin at each other
        across the USA.
        Knees up around their ears,
        toes in a New Jersey estuary,
        toes in San Francisco Bay,
        they lift a flap of Hwy
        in their fists
        and shake it up and down.
          . . .

I race beneath white clouds
    crossing the Middle West:
black cow in square beige field,
A&W hamburg,
muddy Missouri,
sweet alfalfa,
    long green beachhead, fixed in time.

On my 25th crossing
        South Dakota becomes more
than the flat name of one state,
        tells itself
in the sound of two words:

"Sou ... sou ..."
        wind fallen into hollows
        for night rest
        after racing all day across corn.

"eth ..."
        the long watery throat of the Missouri,
        fat with mud grains,
        seethes across fallen cottonwood.

"Da — kota"
stea — dy
        crack hand on the bow,
        pheasant in the corn row.

"Da — kota"
        comes smooth and even
        as you drive —
        the way breath comes
        when you lie on your back.
                . . .
White clouds over Dakota
        shift,
        quicken within
        my brain.
The car
        booms
        into hot summer wind.

        Between my eyes
        a soft explosion:

Those clouds
are painted on!

You could chip them off
with your fingernails.

I ask my hitchhiker,
"What's behind flat clouds?"
Nodding his lion's mane,
he rubs his young pug
and begins to discuss
existentialism:
leaving me
with the mutter of clouds...

As a child
I fancied I created sky
by breathing out as I was born.
At twelve
earth continued, circles that opened,
spirals that pivoted, sky that breathed
with its own blood-throb.

And once before the neo-cortex
wrapped itself around, I
roamed ocean gardens as a fish—
spawned, sucked and bit—
till death swallowed me whole.
I had no intellect, with
which to swallow death.

Now traveling
with death
too fast,
my mind is strict
with clouds:
I fear and need the wholeness
of living sky.

...

I ignore my friend
    discussing despair
at the wheel.

    I tell myself a story:

        Once a woman moved to Heron Lake, Minnesota,
        with her twin lilies
        and a golden retriever.
        Heron Lake lipped along all summer,
        syrupy, with many eyes floating in it,
        including the woman's eyes.
        But one day Heron Lake iced over,
        glass of winter, coat of wind;
        the woman saw a single frozen face,
            wearing thin:
        so she and her jeep headed for I-45
        to chase the road's end.

                . . .

Highway
tentacles:
    along them cities,
    towers, walls of schools,
    plastic palm trees,
    wastebaskets that shine in the dark.
No wonder I see
    the backdrop sky
as man-made.

Some people
    who claim
everything is "like"
    something,
say even the sky
    can be jailed in a word;
they resent Ocean.

What does it think it's doing,
    Ocean,
being like nothing else
    before or since?
Incomparable, unregistered,
    won't speak when spoken to.

On a high bridge over Chicago
    my car's small shadow
obliterates the metal scratches
    on the rind of earth.
500 thousand people tried
    to put Illinois in order
but lost to the rivers and the swamp.

II

On the road, I keep rocks:
    The *Love Poems* of Pablo Neruda,
    The Dying Self by Charles Fair,
    and *The Poetics of Space* by Gastón Bachelard.
I keep
    a blood-red rock from the Midwest,
    a flat grey rock from Plum Island, Massachusetts,
    and a milk-white Pacific rock with a thumb-sized hole.
I arrange these
in an order that suits my mood
at each stop.
    I pause over the milk-white rock:
        It wants to be near the others
        but far enough
        for its own dense thoughts.

At sunset
a tall dark ranger
on a California beach
stopped to admire
my bronze belly, apricot ears,
the way I recited "yes."
He asked me to dinner.

He turned out to be interested in
throwing girls into swimming pools
while other girls watched.
So I walked home alone
through an orange orchard
reciting "yes,"
       and found the milk-white rock.
It is a horse's skull, rising through fog;
it is the fish head
I was, before
I was born,
the face with one eye
who stared at me
from my womb
when I traveled inside, by dream.

Out of flailing gravel roads,
     flower rivers,
officials of gate and street and pulpit
     gesturing:
out of roads cut for the first time
     through alfalfa fields,
out of the freakish luster of freeway slabs,
     when I don't see anyone I know all day,
or any place I've slept before,
     comes the ordering
     of rocks.

          . . .

In this world
    which has been all day
    scattering and gathering,
my car
    is my cave,
the engine my fire.
    The rear exhaust
gives the world the finger.

My car smiles at me
    through chrome braces
when I emerge from an unfriendly restaurant.
    It's an adolescent,
half girl, half boy, shiny red,
    bugging everybody.

When I shift, I make letters,
L   H   U   and   O.
Devious Boston streets register
polysyllabic words, complex sentences.
New York City elicits
an abrupt, thrusting language.
Country roads in Dakota
transcribe long and clean.

I ride, an eye, staring
    from the bone socket of my car.
The land flies by in slivers
    under heavy rain.
Hail pounds the skull,
    but I curl
on red seats
    and spin my wheels.

III

Every morning
    I sever the umbilical cord
grown during the night
    between myself and the moon.
I learn to trust the moon
    more than any human face.
Its eye returns each midnight
    to follow my story,
folds inward once a month
    upon its own saga.

I identify
    with things going long distances
alone:
    the ant on the silo
    the eagle on the wind.

But I can't stop eavesdropping:

"Nice day!" "let 'er rip!" "hi ya!"
    "right on" "Amen" "holy haystacks"
        "faster'n shit through a goose."

I'm caught by features:
    vanilla dairy-queen hair-do,
        blue thread of seaweed throbbing
            at a baby's throat.

Overtaken by voices:
    ice-creaking-on-the-lake voice,
        steak-beaten-until-tender voice,
            oily black-olive voice.

Forced to remember
    the Texas country woman
    who mauls and heals
    her innocent soft-nosed son
    with her gutteral voice and her downy voice,
    pinching his arms, spooning gravy into his mouth.

In Boston a woman with one leg shorter than the other
    talks to a posh green lamp post.

In Las Vegas a man with vodka veins
    screeches for his panting husky to FETCH.

A Navaho boy lopes across the desert near The Big Rock
    Candy Mountain, stretching to catch a frisbee.

In Carmel, California, two men try to drown a duck
    with their kayaks. One has a seaweed toupee on
    his bald head.

Every Sunday in Ames, Iowa, an old lady with two
    invisible Indians flanking her, marches to church.

I try to be metal,
    a man-made node,
but the retarded child in Howard Johnson's
    eats cheesecake,
gesturing to herself
    in cream language
and I must
do as I please to her
with my eyes
    while she does
    what she can
    with her inherited self.

IV

During an afternoon rainstorm in spring
    I stood musing with ghosts
at a stranger's attic window.
    Now on the road, I remember
I left the window open.

Which thoughts left behind
    have escaped?
How long will they ghost from mind to mind
    looking for their source?

                Once I lived on Heron Lake, Minnesota.
                I sang like a cricket
                about an acre of earth
                that made its home in my body —
                through the food I grew,
                through the same dirt day after day
                under bare feet.
                At four in the afternoon
                every 10th of October,
                a certain slant of sun
                radiated gloom and cheer
                from the hearts of past Octobers.

On the road
    I am a hunter.
I salt the game I catch
    and carry it
over many rivers.
    I weave my song
with the skeins
    of many soils.

I lick time.
        The car licks up
white dashes.
        I unravel
but cradle some core
        of myself,
as each new place
        jogs my wheel.

When I need to cry out,
        I call on
something hungry
        that endures:
it roars like an ocean
        packed into a point of space,
a vacuum
        filling with all life.

Hawks circle
        in blue gaps between the Black Hills;
the flatlands of Iowa
        roll out of the Mississippi roll.
People shout and march
        along the super-freeways.
I speed away from them.
        Slow times
when I choose no one
        are vital
to the stone I smooth inside.

V

I stop longest
in the flattest, most solitary space:
out in the middle
of the Middle West.

Let the clouds move, let them run.
I hold out both arms,
laughing my basic
prairie laugh,
my friendly
cornstalk-rustling laugh
(the laugh I hide in cities)
which invites every black and white rapist
to come across the Rockies and Alleghenies
and up from the Delta
and eat my corn.

How far do you think they'd get?
eating their way,
burrowing black and white tunnels
into the wide yellow fields,
the big golden tummy of my Ma,
mama USA.
"Stop that tickling," I'd say,
"I got plenty."

. . .

The power in the stone
I smooth within me
grows.
    In Oregon
my forehead broadens,
new wrinkles flowing with rivers of sweat.
    In Kansas
I stroke row on row
of gold wheat sprouted on my thighs.
    In Wyoming
my heart leaps: the Tetons!
those tall ones who will stand up
next to me.

    From the 6th tier
of a Boston Celtics basketball game
one night
I look down,
and the thousands let go,
recoil
into my eyes,
like the geography map the 4th grade teacher
used to snap up
over the blackboard.
    I am a map
snapped back into myself,
filling with stadiums of people,
lines, teams,
choruses of people.

I feel so big,
a road hog
        spinning my wheel,
writing
        to empty my pocket gopher cheeks,
writing
        to restore my normal size,
writing
        till I drive to my own bones.

I'll stop
someday
        and leave my car, dead,
        in a graveyard of cars:
American in America
        traveling
the road.

And I'll leave my skeleton
to protect these pages,
this black on white map,
        this heart given voice to,
        this hunger fed.